A THAMES BESTIARY
Peter Hay & Geoff Sawers

"Dissolv'd beneath whose potent stroke
The flint a torrent gave;
Who spake; and from the yielding rock
Gush'd forth the bidden wave."
Psalm 114
(James Merrick's paraphrase, 1776)

"Dulce est desipere in loco."
Horace

GU00802234

Some of these poems have been previously published, in the following journals (UK, except where stated): *Ambivalent, Asinine, Asparagus, Babbitt's Belfry, Billets-Doux* (Senegal), *Bunty, A Case of Celery, The Danegeld, The Dartmouth Naval Review, Decompositions, Docked Wages, Echo, Echo, Egyptian Camera, El Niño, Engage, Envoi, Epithet, Ersatz, Facile Trash, Fossil Guns, Gaudete, Gimcrack, Girdle, Glottal-stop, Grand Panjandrum, Haggis* (Australia), *Halitosis, Impotent Gods, Ju-ju, Just 17, Kelpie, The Lady's Companion, Laryngitis, Lungfish, My Feet, Mo' Wax!, Nabob, Nachschlag, Negatur, Orange Pie, Poetry Salzburg Review* (Austria), *Pump, Queen Anne's Abdication, Roundyhouse, The Saigon Daily Chronicle, Salami* (Belgium), *Scrofulous Stygian Gloom, The Tablet, The Tabloid, The Taffrail, The Unruly Sun, War Cry, Welter-weight, Zimmerframe Pile-up* and *Zombie Drummers*; some of which actually exist. Our thanks to the editors thereof.

Two Rivers Press
35–39 London Street
Reading RG1 4PS

© 2007 Jill Hay, Geoff Sawers
The Coypu drawing on page 42 is by Mick Sparksman, circa 1978.
Thanks to Ruth and Joe Sparksman for permission to reprint it.
Many thanks to John Froy for badgering this book into existence.

ISBN 978-1-901677-50-8

Designed by Goober Fox and typeset in Berthold Walbaum 9/12
Printed on Cyclus Offset recycled paper by CPI Antony Rowe

Two Rivers Press is a member of Inpress

CONTENTS

FOWLS OF THE AIR

BEE

You busy? Nah, not really. Just supping at a pint o' Brakspears outside the Dreadnought. Ignoring the warnings of Weil and Verlaine, we strip to our shorts and dive into the Thames, shocking cool even on a summer's day. We submerge, our eyes, ideas, identities, in the murmur of bees and dream of honey, read Yeats' Isle of Innisfree. When a bee-keeper dies a swarm will beard his house. We dream of being stung; wake up swollen, stiff and sore.

BLACKCAP

1ˢᵗ May 1998

Car park shrubs, a spirit warbles
in the glistening rain of new burst leaf.
Sweet wet sip of bubbling song.

Everything flows. When the bed of the river Kennet at Reading Gas Works was dug up during the summer of 1880 they found bones of beaver, boar and wolf. In February 1993 I was amazed to see a male Blackcap in the trees by Blake's Lock. A bird that I had always only known as a summer visitor to Britain in the deep mid-winter seemed concrete evidence of Global Warming–first a myth, this slowly became accepted fact and then came into question again. Our wintering black-caps turned out to be refugees from harsh winters in Eastern Europe; nothing is so simple. Everything flows–especially rivers. What will the Thames look like in a hundred years' time? Will we see crocodiles crowding the papyrus beds at Richmond? It might add some spice to the boat race–no more throwing the winning cox in–maybe the losing one. You can't step twice in the same day.

The commonest gull throughout the region. Merely a dark smudge behind the ear in winter, they get the full dark-chocolate hood in breeding plumage. Also the communist gull. During the 1960s and 70s their inland spread in Great Britain began to cause serious alarm among free-market ornithologists. Their promiscuous interchangeability was feared to be a threat to individual freedom. Attempts were undertaken to isolate and track particular gene stocks among the Black-headed Gulls of the Thames Valley. All failed, of course. These guys stick together: apian solidarity.

BOAT RACE

The collective noun for a large
   group of swans is a regatta

A fluff of cygnets
A squabble of coots

A mist of mayflies
A glamour of fireflies

A rump of hampers
A sheer of skiffs

A rumble of boatmen
A rage of oars

An inanity of undergraduates
A cosh of Pimms

An absence of corncrakes
A ball of rooks

BANDED DAMSELFLY

hammerhead sharps
ziggurat sickles
busy as cars

COCKEREL

Here's the edge of the world–
lichen, quartz, witches.
The cliff awaits your drop.
But even if you should jump
the wind would still hurl you back
like a rag into blackthorn
impale you on a weather vane
where you could crow forever.

His breast is a map of the Empire. Burns like a beacon on the holly bush. In Spring he turns the colour of Kitchener's cap. Sometimes seen marshalling trains in the GWR sidings, the cock linnet is not a bird to be disobeyed.

COOT

That testy hermit who had spent
nine years in his cell trying to devise
a mathematical symbol for chaos

gave up, burnt his nibs
and shaved his head, took coot form,
and staked a patch

of river by Isleworth mill.
Cute little black boot of a vicar.
Fulica does not eat corpses

nor does he gad aboot
flapping about in different directions
as the heretics do

it's not their fault
but they're shrill and ridiculous
silly dabblers and bobbling babblers

spoiling for a fight
then they run away, and like Jesus Christ
walk on the water.

Milton's Satan appeared as a Cormorant. Many people are struck by the reptilian look of the bird. Others have seen it, its wings stretched out to dry after a dive, as an emblem of Christ crucified. Perhaps the Cormorant, like Saint Paul, is all things to all men?

Lentic predator. Spread throughout the British Isles with the rail and canal networks during the Industrial Revolution. No one knows where they lived before, due to scarcity of detailed records, although the Roman aqueductial system may well have been a favourite. You can tell Daubenton's even in flight from the slightly smaller and commoner Pipistrelle by its less flickering, more strongly swooping flight. Also known as Brunel's bat.

There was a famous radio broadcast one night
   from an orchard by the river near Hampton Court.
A nightingale in the apple trees, out of sight,

traded riffs and refrains with a man on the decks—
   scratching, squealing, twittering, booming bass,
mingling his liquid burble with stabs of T.Rex.

People turned off their sets, came out to applaud.
   A BBC van nearby cut the Queen to transmit it—
thousands listened, but nobody pressed *Record.*

DRAGONFLY

Often described as indicators of environmental purity, dragonflies can be surprisingly robust. I have seen the hawker *Gomphus vulgatissimu*s emerging from the waters of the Thames at Broken Brow, fifty yards from a busy main road; once I saw an Emperor (*Anax imperator*) breezing noisily down Broad Street in Oxford. A design that works, works: dragonflies predate us, they'll clatter over our concrete graves.

Giordano Bruno[1] thought that when the nine nymphs of the river Thames were gathered, a sacred urn would open of its own accord, the nine would become the nine Illuminati, and the ancient creed of the Egyptians would be restored to sweep away the Wars of Religion and bring harmony to the world. Which sounds pretty good. I have never yet counted more than eight species of nymph in Thames waters at any one time, but I live in hope.

1 See *De gli eroici furori* (1585)

Ducks in winter form Parliaments on open water, especially gravel pits, gossiping, factioning, nattering and plotting, but all of this is ultimately pointless. Come spring they will fly north again, and forget everything they planned. Who really cares about holiday friends?

GOLDFINCH

The itchy flight of a finch
                         caught my eye one morning
as I gazed on paradise.
                         Goldfinches howk the heart out of you
but somehow you always forgive them
                         ask them back in your life again.

Sometimes you have to look at the world
                         like it's the first day of spring–
then flit to the next bare thistle.
                         Finches taught me that.

GREAT CRESTED GREBE

freezing fog
   a glassy frostwork morning
      and I heard a sneeze, dainty as a duchess
      and turned and saw no one
   but her, slender and coy
turning away

HELOPHILUS PENDULUS

How hard it is to eulogise a fly
And one with such a cumbersome name–
  but this was beautiful
and I sank up to my chin among the
  lilies and reeds
in the water suddenly deep
  at the edge of Dinton lake
and the hot June sun raised a
humming all around
and a large fly, striped, like a
humbug or a baby grebe,
flew, hovered, flew, hovered,
hovered before my face,
finally dismissed me, and went on its own way.

HERON

"I saw a young man come one night
an apple in his hand
by moonlight and candlelight
we find the mollhern land

I saw a young stag come one night
All weeping bitterly
By moonlight and candlelight
We find the gallows tree..."

Old Twyford folk-song

The heron waxes and wanes with the passing month. From the horns of a wintry new moon she creeps, lean and angular, to the flooded meadows to gorge on sodden moles. Stiff as a standpipe in a drought, creaking in the wind; battleship grey. An east wind sharp as flint resurrects baby pterosaurs from the Thames-side swamp. This cold Siberian blast brings the Surrey traffic of the slow circling stack of aircraft waiting to land at Heathrow, a low repressed whine and moan, a dangling kind of flight, head-lights lighting up the rusted flanks of the gasometer. Normally it's whoosh and off to the western yonder, a roar and gone. But tonight they're circling, lights in the sky, heavy and ponderous and so low, like giant rays, I swear I see their wings flap.

And then under a fat buttery moon the heron waits by the riverside, solitary beaky paunchy scholar, digesting the daylight. The frogs' evil God, as plump as sin. Local tradition links the heron with St Barham, patron saint of the muddled and indecisive.

JACKDAWS

Jack-knifing, corkscrewing,
fooling about,
cranky savants crazy in the gale.

One flaps past on its back
then pulls out a stop.
They're taking it in turns

showing off then regrouping in a flock,
ack-acking back
to the factory towers.

JAY

wears flash rings, initialled 'J'
costa del sol gangsta
his villa a warm pink,
an aqua splash of blue his pool,
and somewhere
the loot, the cash.

KINGFISHER

'It is a very common Experiment, by striking with a Flint against a steel, to make certain fiery and shining sparks to fly out from between those two compressing Bodies..'

Robert Hooke – Micrographia, 1665

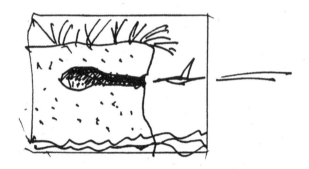

An instant of combustion. Thought visualised. The oxy-acetylene arc that cuts you free from the wreckage of your life. Tonight autumn stuns with a flare of stars, a peacock fan of eyes. I am staring at the pilot light of the central heating. It is blue and barely wavers.

MAGPIES

You don't want to mess with magpies. Their chequered careers are ready to spook you, clattering across your path in superstitious destiny, safe as killer whales in their two-tone power suits, glittering eyes alert to the thieving chance, nasty neighbours eating your babies, tarred and whitewashed as warning. Dazzlers, they give no quarter, attack a cat. Two for joy, amigo, two for joy.

MALLARD

Milord Draco
in white neck-tie /
    neck ringed with brine
home from iridescent
emerald seas
his golden prow
dabbling pondwater
quaking the main

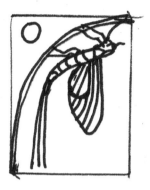

Ephemera species. There were husks all over the narrow-boat. They stuck to the tacky paint that blazing day. You could never get rid of them, sand as you might. Then you sold the boat. They are probably still there, wherever it is. Ephemera.

Common Quaker

Moths are pathos.
Modest ghosts of pale discretion,
   the empty husks you find
clearing rooms, behind the paintings …

These folded brittle papyrus deltas once were
each a human soul. You prop them up on the windowsill
to catch the last rays of winter sun, and feel them
   crumble …

Foxed folios, spored fungii, bedstraw, brocade,
Sallows, Foresters, Quakers, Lackeys, and Footmen;
the Ambiguous, the Suspected, the Dismal.

PIGEONS

Purring, pooting
Pompeii's pumice
dust in the dovecote.

Squab for the pot. We opened doors
to a monsoon terrace
a clap of doves.

Rainbow nacre.
Their wings sheet white
against thunder cloud.

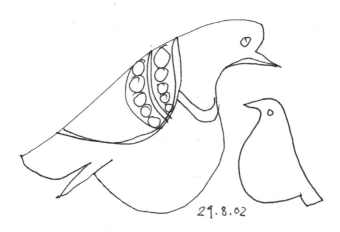

29.8.02

A curious relic of the poet Arthur Rimbaud has survived his restless travels. A hand-written scrap dating from the brief period of his residence in Reading in 1874:

homing–working–fantails
pearl-eyed tumbler–
shortfaced–performing tumblers
trumpeters–squeakers
blue, red turbits–Jacobins
baldpates–pearl eyes–tumbles well
high flying performing tumblers
plashed–rough legged
grouse limbed
black buglers
saddle back
over thirty tail feathers

Such specific information leads us to speculate that the *enfant terrible* had become a peaceable pigeon-fancier. Who knows? Perhaps he had read in the Reading Observer of 7th November that year: "It is proposed to hold a Pigeon and English and Foreign Cage Bird show early in February … any ladies or gentlemen taking an interest in the matter … are requested to communicate with Mr F. J. Crapp, 69 Castle Street."

Rimbaud's local, used by both pupils and teachers of the private school where he taught French, still served beer until just a few years back, and perhaps, if you asked when Bob the landlord had had a few himself, a personal derangement of all the senses. It was called 'The Dove'. Oscar Wilde, born four days after (or was it before?) Rimbaud, had a less happy sojourn in the town a few years later–in the gaol, a mere pigeon spit from the Dove. According to Wilde's friend Robert Ross, memory later allowed him to transform his humiliating experience: 'The hideous machicolated towers were already turned into minarets, the very warders into benevolent mamelukes ...' Weirdly, Rimbaud had anticipated this: 'I accustomed myself to simple forms of hallucination. I would actually see a mosque where there was a factory ...' Today there is.

Is it true that in prison Oscar trained a pigeon, called it Arthur, and used it to send poems to Bosie? One of these disputed poems, poignantly titled 'Homing', allegedly describes his former lover as 'pearl-eyed', 'short-faced', and a 'squeaker', but concludes in his favour that he 'tumbles well'.

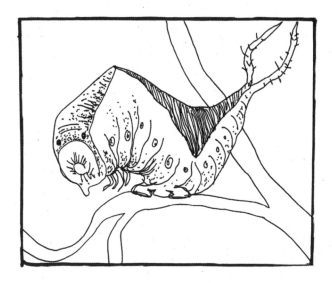

The Puss Moth's desire for willows and poplars makes the sallow banks of the Thames a natural habitat for this fluffy white ghost, named for its screeching 'mieouw' as chloroform snuffs its soul. The net descends in the glare of mercury vapour and the river doesn't hear a thing.

The bright green and black zig-zagged caterpillar in its later larval incarnation wears a mask, a false red face of devilish deception, a warning backed up by two extrudable whips. Under attack, sour Puss Moth larva squirts acid from its mouth. It's only natural. We all do. Come May, let's creep up on them one night. Stroke them until they purr. Take them home for breeding.

31

RED KITE

Welcome home, if home there be,
   for a peripatetic scrounger.
Once you snatched toys from children,
   herring from housewives,
a feathered cap from me.

Then retired for some centuries' hermitage
somewhere around Llandeilo
and returned, purified, and stronger,
   met on the ledge.

Now barcode slabs shimmer above Playhatch
or Christmas Common, wedged tails, aerofoil tilts
of wing catch the sun, revealing bright red.
   No strings attached.

SONG THRUSH

clattering consonant scales
in hedgerows the thrush still sings
in some ancient, near-forgotten british tongue

sunlight on grass and oil

Sociable birds, just like sociable fish, are mad for their personal space. Even in huge migration flocks they seem to have some kind of sixth sense or repulsive force that prevents them from colliding with each other. In fact, bird flocks naturally sort themselves into something resembling a molecular crystal lattice. Some birds stack in neat rows and columns, others in complex tessellating polyhedra. Urban starlings form a pseudo-ferrous matrix, each body mass held at a regular 1.78 wing-breadths from the next, and despite the extreme warp and torsion undergone as the flock turns in flight, or settles on a municipal building, they never—that is, *never*—collide.

SWALLOW

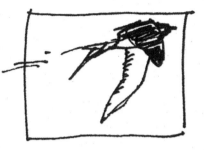

The theory of evolution would have had us believe that life is in itself marvellous and awe-inspiring. But, like the hirundo, we are really all made of clay. Each of us has a divine hair on our head that we must guard with vigilance. Beware: should a swallow pluck this hair, you are doomed to eternal perdition. Let the weak bewail their loss. What happened to the hundreds, literally *hundreds*, of swallow nests that were counted a generation ago under the bridge at Clifton Hampden? I guess they just had to go. Wake up. It's a war.

SWAN

Olor is no colour
a shining white piece of paper
awaiting lines and received tenets
transmigration of the soules of men
    into the bodies
of beasts most suitable unto their
    humane condition.

Orpheus the musician became a swan.
Have you ever heard one sing?
Aldrovandus observed the sinuous revolution
a serpentine and trumpet recurvation of the Weazon
and by the figure thereof a musical modulation effected.

They also say that in the Northern parts of the world
once the lute players have tuned up
a great many swans are invited in
and they play a concert together in strict measure.

Wuup wee wuup wee wuup wee WUUP & a lisping whistle
as wings beat the resistant river air
sometimes a serpentine hiss as they land
and then the hushed feathered silence
of their sublime arrogance.

In the town of Cirencester in 1648, whilst King Charles I was being held prisoner by Parliament, a group of Royalist noblemen gathered in secret to toast the King's fortune. One man rose to stand the toast, when a swallow flew into the room through the open window and perched on the lip of the earthenware cup. The whole gathering paused in silence. The bird dipped the tip of its tiny beak into the liquid, sipped, and then spat the wine back into the cup and flew out again.

Shocked and dispirited by this negative omen, the group disbanded. Some, seeking allegiance with the sharp dark powers of the swift, crafted sweeping assassins' daggers from obsidian that had been secretly collected on the slopes of Sicily's Mount Etna and then just disappeared from the face of the earth. The more homely among them were content to see out their years by moulding small lumps of clay, in homage both to the humbler house martin and to the process of God's creation.

TERN

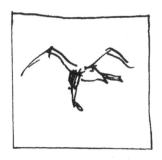

Terns are so bolshie that you frequently find shyer birds like the Little Ringed Plover nesting among a colony of terns to protect their young from the crows. Life among the sweet and tender hooligans. Who first called them sea swallows? They'll slit the sea asunder, but never swallow it.

WOOD WARBLER

Five inches of firelight. Throat throbbing with song. A trail of five-pence pieces into your palm. In the oak and beech tops pairs hunt for food, almost invisible from the ground.

BEASTS OF THE FIELD

Cold, they're coiled like a squeezed blackhead. Sunshine, they're off, rubbing the warm earth, sashaying and pulsing, fattening to strike. Lies, all lies. Medusa the seducer shakes her pretty locks, accountants tot their tills, snake-oil merchants strut their stump, and viper zig-zags into hiding.

At Dorchester-on-Thames there's a bell to repel all serpents. It's called Big Dong. Tenor-toned, it was cast in Wokingham with the stamp of a dragon, and presented to the church in 1380 by Ralph Retwold. The bell is dedicated to St. Birinus, the local saint who had come from Milan to convert the King of Wessex. As Dorchester's first Bishop, Birinus controlled a diocese extending to the Northumbrian border yet he was undone, not martyred, but killed by a snake-bite.

So, be careful if you wear sandals. However, the dying Birinus pronounced immunity to snakebite for his flock: 'Stay within the sound of my church bells and you'll be protected'. A ploughman ventured to Wallingford, found everyone dead, their feet swollen purple with poison, all the alabaster effigies in the churches scraped as smooth as eggs in futile search for an antidote. Since then the good Dorchester folk have never strayed.

BADGER

Shaggy digger, trundler, snuffler;
trufflehunter of the deep wild wood–
daylight narcoleptic,
we keep on seeing you squashed,
and wonder how your cubs survive
when you don't come home to ground.
We once spread honey and digestives
on leaves and twigs around a sett,
went away, crept back,
settled downwind, itchy, quiet.
Waited long for you to come out,
push a stripy snout into failing light.

This whacking great rodent was the subject of a regular cartoon strip in the Waveney Clarion back in the mid 1970s. The hero was a beleaguered bargee in cloth cap and braces, and the coypu (of whom there was at the time a well-established breeding colony near Slough) a Baader–Meinhof-style gang of freedom-fighters. They had brought Marxism to the Berkshire meadows along with their furs and their gangsters' molls. Britain's last wild-bred coypu was run down by a battered old Vauxhall estate on the B376 near Datchet, the same week the Belgrano went down. Margaret Thatcher claimed the victory as a personal one for herself.

FROG

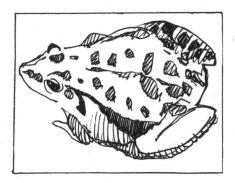

From Ashton Keynes to Rotherhithe
from a seething jelly to a tiger's flea
from your ear to Basho's puddle
from a bigger splash to a tenor bellow
brag, sweet frog from the shallows.
Your time is surely here.

The myths are strong. The psychology of lust still ripples through the grass and into the water. Snakes raise the hairs on your neck, bring out the worst in you. You want to trap that fork-tongued slithering wavelength with a cleft stick, pitch it into a sack. But you can barely even touch it–if you do, you find that it is really a lamb. The nearest you usually get is finding a sloughed skin; when you were seventeen you wrapped one around your neck and went to a Sisters of Mercy gig. For once you got respect. For one night only.

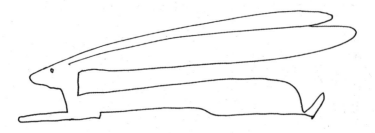

The hare was introduced to these islands in the iron age by Brythonic tribes migrating from Central Europe, who thought it was a kind of mis-shapen, edible cat. A mistake realised soon enough. The hare keeps the earth flat merely by virtue of his own velocity.

Lazy athlete. Startled sinew. Nose all a-quiver.

Some people are always up on their high horse. Horsey people. Not necessarily big-nosed, but maybe a curl, a flare to their nostrils which take in big gulps of air to propel their principled thoughts in a gallop of speech. I like them, obey them, they're fun. Ouch! That leather whip, the smell of sweat. 'C'mon, climb on up and ride.'

Then there's the anatomists, admirers of flesh, George Stubbs and all the punters shouting at shampoo adverts, a flick of the mane as shiny flanks crash through waves. The breeders, the owners, the jockeys. Epona! Books written about this. Lifetimes devoted. Girls smitten.

46

Within his dreams and visions, Swedenborg understood the estimable equus as a symbol for intellectual principle. Not only for its speed, nobility and loyalty but also for a deductive strategy—somehow ascribing the device of the Trojan Horse to the animal's intelligence rather than to the mere men who planned that simulacrum. The hooves of this high-minded horse strike the flinty ground to break open fountains of truth. And souls travel on horseback to the land of the dead. The Bestiarists at least knew something about the horse and for once demonstrated some empirical sense and refined appreciation, naming figure, beauty, merit and colour as four necessary qualities for good breeding. Colour is discussed in some detail: "... bay, golden, ruddy, chestnut, deer-coloured, pale yellow, grey, roan, hoary, silver, white, flea-bitten, black ..."

Neck rippling like a basket of eels, protected by clustered brass suns to reflect the evil eye, the big vulgar clumper hauls his load along the Thames and the sides of the Horseshoe Bridge are raised to deflect his fear of heights and water. Barges full of hay sail below.

mole or freckle?
just below the eye
clustered on the cheek
constellating the neck

their little heaps
dot the chalk scarp
where the white horse
is getting grey.

By the riverbank just south of the major Bracknell-Marlow fault[2]
there is an extraordinary Quaternary submerged forest, home
to an unique and distinctive fauna. Microfossil age determina-
tion using conodonts suggests that the entire sequence has been
inverted; and for sure, deep quarrying in the 1980s did indeed
uncover a fossilized tractor several metres *below* an incomplete
diplódocus. The crows in this area have been observed flying

2 A classic strike-slip, say some authorities–an hallucination, say others.
See particularly Danaos, Timothy (1968) and Doña Ferrentes (2006).

upside-down; cock robins frequently sing their autumn song in spring, and vice-versa; there are unconfirmed but persistent rumours of a colony of arboreal moles. It's a topsy-turvy place. Civil servants go there to lose their inhibitions, teenage joy-riders to gain some. Seven members of a New-age convoy that settled nearby subsequently joined the RAF. Unsurprisingly, it is not marked on any map.

 An otter is half mouse, half cat, half ghost, and a bit of an eel. Several souls inhabit each slick body. No one ever sees an otter, they just infer from the dainty spraints he leaves under river bridges that he has graced us with his presence.

Slippery, spicy, bouncing, ballocking
          down the path at eventide
                    into a brown study.

The rabbit was also introduced to these islands: by the Normans, once they discovered that the hares introduced before ran too fast. Rabbits grow like small orange-trees, ever-fruitful, multiplying like trekkie tribbles. Suffocate all other herbivorous life under the sheer bulk of their cuteness. But foxes have to eat as well.

SLOW WORM

On an orchid bank near Pangbourne strewn with wild strawberry, self-heal, and St John's-wort, you found a dead slow worm. High summer: the first day of July. At first you thought it was just a cast-off skin, but you felt the weight of it as you picked it up, and an ant crawled from the eye-socket. You found yourself actually scared of the thing—like it could do anything.

"Katesgrove [in Reading] had long been famous for its excavations ... The Spider, however, over-topped all else. It is recorded that during some digging a flint had been cracked, and from out of the middle of the flint walked a spider ... For how many millions of years that patient spider had been awaiting release from its captivity was a cause for many disputes ..."

Leslie Harman, 'Parish of St. Giles-in-Reading', 1946

'Send me a cool rut-time,
Jove, or who can blame me
to piss my tallow?'
The Merry Wives of Windsor

Staggering home in the dawn, mere men rattling their chains, blasted askew, links in the family tree riven by lightning, branches severed, their antler crowns suffering the mockery accorded to cuckolds.

Woden, Windsor and the Wild Hunt.
Herne, Horn and Heron. Hounds.
                              Tally ho
                              hellwain
Grimnir, wolves, pitch of night, chains, ravens,
creaking wagons, midwinter, storms, shrieking,
shouting, baying, yelping, barking, bells ringing
swords clashing, neighing, stamping, wind blast
drunkards, rowdies, ballad mongers, cheats
jangling, clanking
deformed deer heads, faces in their chests, headless
maimed, entrails spilling, luminous, fiery,
howls of pain, cawk, cawk, breathing flames
saddles stuck with red hot nails
rascals, busybodies, pranksters, bounders

A rag bag army raving and howling, black horses pounding, all that corny horny carny hieronymous hell stuff–the hunt. And aloof, elegant and most intelligent–the white hart. It was in Windsor Forest–a dawn drive, down a little dip and up a rise, mist still lingering and, in the middle of the road, stock still a white stag. He turns to look at us in our metal box, then walks off into the fog. You don't forget things like that.

Cryptozoology's hot this season
as are Jacobean pamphlets
with provincial imprints:
Christies are quietly confident.

Imperfectly printed on rough rag paper
from blocks of contemporary English oak
the scholars try to treat it as a joke

but can't deny the identification
of an upright, club-tailed, boxing-gloved clown:
a Red Kangaroo at the gates of the town.

They complain that the watermark isn't local;
that the sole known copy, now in the hands
of a reclusive collector with a villa in Cannes

can no longer be studied—that may be so
but parish accounts for the month of June
sixteen hundred and twenty two

detail payments at the close of the fair
to a foreign prize-fighter with a big broad tail:
three barrels of oats, wrapped up in a sail.

What's got into me? We need to slow down. God, we are ugly. I'm a fat prick. A toad. Feel my warty bumps. My swollen ego. The air beneath my earthy skin. Look into my ruby eye and be excused from all duties. I'll be crucified for you, slow in exercise, encrusted with the microscopic jewels of life; puffed up, inflated by the desire of strangers. I'm your familiar. Family. Let's get out of this.

On hot August days in Slough town centre you can see dozens of water beetles landing on the car roofs and twirling furiously before taking off again. Metallic paint, blue lake, deepest space.

FISHES OF THE RIVER

Eels are always a metaphor for something else. No-one ever lets them be themselves.

 In the terrible winter of 1125 eels left the icy rivers in droves, making nests in barns and haystacks upon dry ground, often dozens all together. The frozen bundles were chipped out by hungry peasants with chisels; a kind of slimy manna. Centuries later the discovery of the humble British eel's remarkable life-cycle started a craze for holidaying in the Caribbean. It became patron fish of the samba and calypso; not an honour it had ever sought for itself. Yet what *is* an eel really? Does anyone know?

CARP

The carp, like the loach, breeds several times a year. Something, I have never understood what, leads many people to associate the carp with royalty. These days it seems that every other actress from Glenda Jackson and Judi Dench to Cate Blanchett and Helen Mirren gets to play Queen Elizabeth I at some point. A little known fact is that every one who does so gets a tiny tattoo of a carp on her shoulder. It is not usually visible in the final edit.

"Porpoises come up above London nearly every year. The first I saw were two above Hammersmith Bridge early on that momentous May morning in 1886, when Mr. Gladstone's First Home Rule Bill was thrown out. I had been up with a friend to hear the result of the division, and had seen the wild joy which followed its announcement in the lobby, and then walked home at dawn and so met the early porpoises. A few years later a fine grampus was found one night lying half-dead by the bows of one of the torpedo-boat destroyers at Chiswick."

'The Naturalist on the Thames', C. J. Cornish, 1902

Many of the Medieval Chronicles note the arrival of cetaceans in the Thames; they were generally thought to be signs from God of his favour[3]. This wondrous aspect did not, of course, prevent them from being hunted down and killed–indeed the prevailing attitude seemed to be that such wonders were sent by the Lord as a boon that it would be blasphemous not to catch. A dolphin was caught in the Thames on Christmas Day, 1392, and four more in 1416. These weren't just dolphins and porpoises, however. Matthew Paris records the catch of a whale, "a monster of prodigious size", at Mortlake in the year 1240. Two 'whirl-pooles', after being chased for two days and nights, were killed at Woolwich in October 1552, and taken for King Edward's inspection. Evelyn's diary records the beaching of two whales, surely either sperm or baleen as both were over 15 metres long, in the Thames around Greenwich in 1658 and then again in 1699.

And a tragic Northern Bottle-nosed Whale caught the public's attention in January 2006; despite frantic rescue attempts it died of dehydration in the Thames in central London. It was thought to be trying to make its way home to the North Atlantic–via Reading and Oxford.

3 The Reading Mercury records on 22nd December 1834 a curious sight for public entertainment: the skeleton of a whale "with nothing in the slightest degree offensive about it".

As Doctor Boteler said of the strawberry: "Doubtless God could have made a finer berry, but doubtless God never did." There is no finer fish than the barbel. Just look at them. Preferably from a low bridge, 500 yards up a clear swift-flowing Thames tributary, down at the barbel waving, holding steady, face to the flow. Just look at them.

PIKE

Aloof, the ugly old baron hangs in the shade.
A great switch of muscle, twelve pounds lean grey meat,
Scabbed and silent and cool.

Let the young play on the greensward in the sun,
he prefers his pavilion of umbelliferous gloom.
He will weigh your eloquence, and your beauty
   against his need.

For years there were rumours of a monstrous pike in the Thames at Remenham. Never actually seen, its existence was deduced from the way that cygnets, young labradors and occasional small boats would be suddenly gulped underwater. Local fisherman Pete Winters claims to have hooked the monster one freezing morning in March 1996, with a leg of mutton on 3-ply climbing rope, but couldn't land the fish. Faced with the sight of its huge jaws on the riverbank in front of him, he simply cut the rope and let it go. A few fish scales of inordinate size on his waders were the only evidence, but Mrs Winters cleaned them before he could alert the press.

TENCH

What do I know?
Just words: tenacious, trenchant, arras, Ypres.
Doctor fish, ministering in the filth.

Unobserved solitary of the lowest depths
the carp's kin–
Tinca tinca,
soldier, spy,
a swallower of keys.

Anglers daub their faces with French mud,
rub their spam-baiting hands
with anise or the stench of ramson.

Tench is too wise and too cautious.

"There appears to be a fascination in gudgeon fishing that is not easy to account for ... however, the fascination certainly exists, and it is mentioned as a fact, that the clergyman of a parish in the neighbourhood of Hampton Court, who was engaged to be married to the daughter of a bishop, enjoyed his gudgeon fishing so much, that he arrived too late to be married, and the lady, offended at his neglect, refused to be united to one who appeared to prefer his rod to herself."

Edward Jesse, An Angler's Rambles, 1836

The chub is a mystical fish. Many years ago it laid a curse on any verbal descripxion of itselfs. To this day it can be delineated only in the most mundane terms: weight, body/muscle ratio, and so on.

Any poets who attempd to eulogixe it are condemned to incoxxhrjsptl. Ewnglltn ap whinnea6hahe fk. Gsotne[n!

TROUT

the rainbow trout glows
like the surface of unpolished metal
he bathes his face in city air

A WORD ON NAMES AND TERMINOLOGY

"... it has been my wish to draw from every source
one thing, the strange phosphorus of the life,
nameless under an old misappelation."
William Carlos Williams, "In the American Grain", 1925

The Misappelation Mountains rise north of the Chilterns near where the Mississippi meets the Tamesos on the Anonymous Plain. Viking explorers raiding from the North-East, among them Linnaeus, reached an impasse here, having run out of words. They buried secret hoards on the gravel ridges as they progressed, but either they were too reduced by malaria to return or they just couldn't remember where they had left the reserve supplies. Dumbstruck by beauty, they struggled to name the many new species of birds and animals they found here. They came up with eight Acks, two Ucks, thirty-three Icks and one It, before meeting the predictable 'Sticky End' somewhere around Benson.

A recent discovery in a garden in Liverpool Road, Reading, suggests that the burials would have been of little sustenance to the plucky explorers. Interred in a small lead box were two chalk tablets, each bearing a hastily scratched 'F'. At best, it would have helped them find an 'If' and an 'Af'. Reports of any similar finds would be welcomed.

INDEX